DRAW 50
DINOSAURS
AND OTHER PREHISTORIC ANIMALS

DRAW 50
DINOSAURS
AND OTHER PREHISTORIC ANIMALS

LEE J. AMES

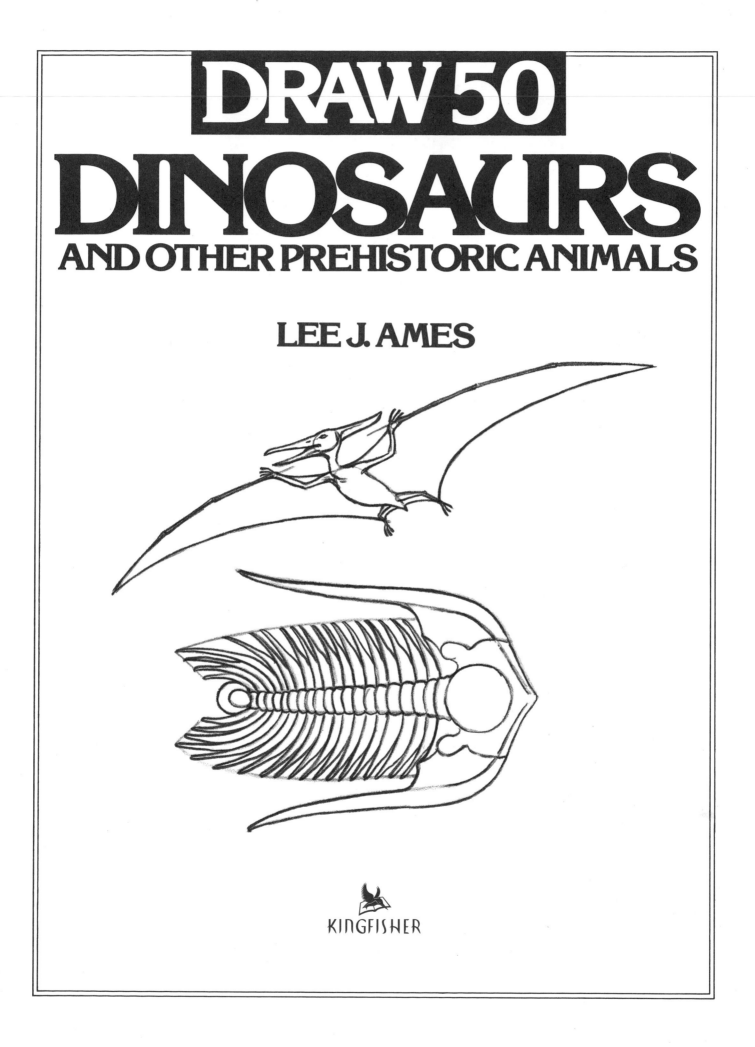

KINGFISHER

KINGFISHER
Kingfisher Publications Plc
New Penderel House, 283-288 High Holborn
London WC1V 7HZ
www.kingfisherpub.com

First published in Great Britain in 1988
by Kingfisher Publications Plc
Originally published in the United States of America in 1977
by Bantam Doubleday Dell Publishing Group, Inc.

20 19 18 17 16 15 14

TS2/0504/AJT/CLSN(HBM)/110WFO/F

A CIP catalogue record for this book
is available from the British Library

ISBN 0 86272 352 3

Phototypeset by Rowland Phototypesetting Limited
Bury St Edmunds, Suffolk
Printed in India

FOREWORD

Mr. Ames has designed a fascinating and instructive book. Young readers and adult students will be able to gain an appreciation of many of nature's now extinct life forms. But, more importantly, they will be able to re-create for themselves the kinds of animals that swam the seas, walked the land and soared through the air in ages long past. Some of these creatures were the ancestors of now living forms, others were only temporarily successful and disappeared without issue. Ponderous woolly mammoths, plated and horned dinosaurs, spiny sharks, flightless birds, membrane-winged reptiles, seagoing lizards, gigantic camels, sabre-toothed cats and giant swimming scorpions all come to life again by way of step-by-step, easy-to-follow instructions. And, although the drawing sequences are very basic and simple, the final results yield scientifically accurate fleshed-out representations of animals known only from their fossil remains. In order to arrive at his reconstructions, the artist has drawn on over a hundred years of scientific research by paleontologists from all over the world. Mr. Ames is to be commended for making the world of prehistoric life accessible to everyone.

GEORG ZAPPLER
Director, Staten Island Zoological Society
(formerly with the Department of Vertebrate Paleontology
The American Museum of Natural History)

TO THE READER

This book will show you a way to draw prehistoric animals. You need not start with the first illustration. Choose whichever you wish. When you have chosen, follow the step-by-step method shown. *Very lightly* and *carefully*, sketch out step number one. However, this step, which is the easiest, should be done most carefully. Step number two is added on top of step number one, also lightly and also very carefully. Step number three is sketched right on top of numbers one and two. Continue in this way until you reach the last step.

It may seem strange to ask you to be extra careful when you are drawing what seem to be the easiest first steps, but this is most important because a careless mistake at the beginning may spoil the whole picture at the end. As you sketch out each step, watch the spaces between the lines, as well as the lines themselves, and see that they are the same. After each step, you may want to lighten your work by pressing it with a plastic, or 'putty' rubber (available at art supply shops).

When you have finished, you may want to redo the final step in India ink with a fine brush or pen – or use a fine pointed felt-tip pen. When the ink is dry, use the plastic rubber to clean off the pencil lines. The rubber will not affect the ink.

Continued over page

Here are some suggestions: In the first few steps, even when all seems quite correct, you might do well to hold your work up to a mirror. Sometimes the mirror shows that you've twisted the drawing off to one side without being aware of it. At first you may find it difficult to draw the egg shapes or circles, or just to make the pencil go where you want it to. Don't be discouraged. The more you practise, the more you will develop control. Use a compass to help you if you wish; professional artists do!

The only equipment you will need will be a medium or soft pencil, paper, the plastic rubber and, if you wish, a compass, pen or brush and India ink – or a felt-tip pen. The first steps in this book are shown darker than necessary so that they can be clearly seen. (Keep your work very light.)

Remember, this book presents only one method of drawing. In a most enjoyable way, it will help you to develop a certain skill and control. But there are many other ways of drawing to which you can apply this skill, and the more of them you try, the more interesting your drawings will be.

Lee J. Ames

TO THE PARENT OR TEACHER

Drawing, like any other skill, requires practice and discipline. But this does not mean that rewards cannot be found along every step of the way.

While contemporary methods of art instruction rightly emphasize freedom of expression and experimentation, they often lose sight of a very basic, traditional and valuable approach: the 'follow me, step-by-step' way that I learned as a youth.

Just as a beginning musician is given simple, beautiful melodies to play, so too the young artist needs to gain a sense of satisfaction and pride in his or her work as soon as possible. The 'do as I do' steps that I have laid out here provide the opportunity to mimic finished images, images the young artist is eager to draw.

Mimicry is prerequisite for developing creativity. We learn the use of our tools through mimicry, and once we have those tools we are free to express ouselves in whatever fashion we choose. The use of this book will help lay a solid foundation for the child, one that can be continued with other books in the *Draw 50* series, or even used to complement different approaches to drawing.

Above all, the joy of making a credible, attractive image will encourage the child to continue and grow as an artist, giving him even more of a sense of pride and accomplishment when his friends say, "Peter can draw a dinosaur better than anyone else!"

Lee J. Ames

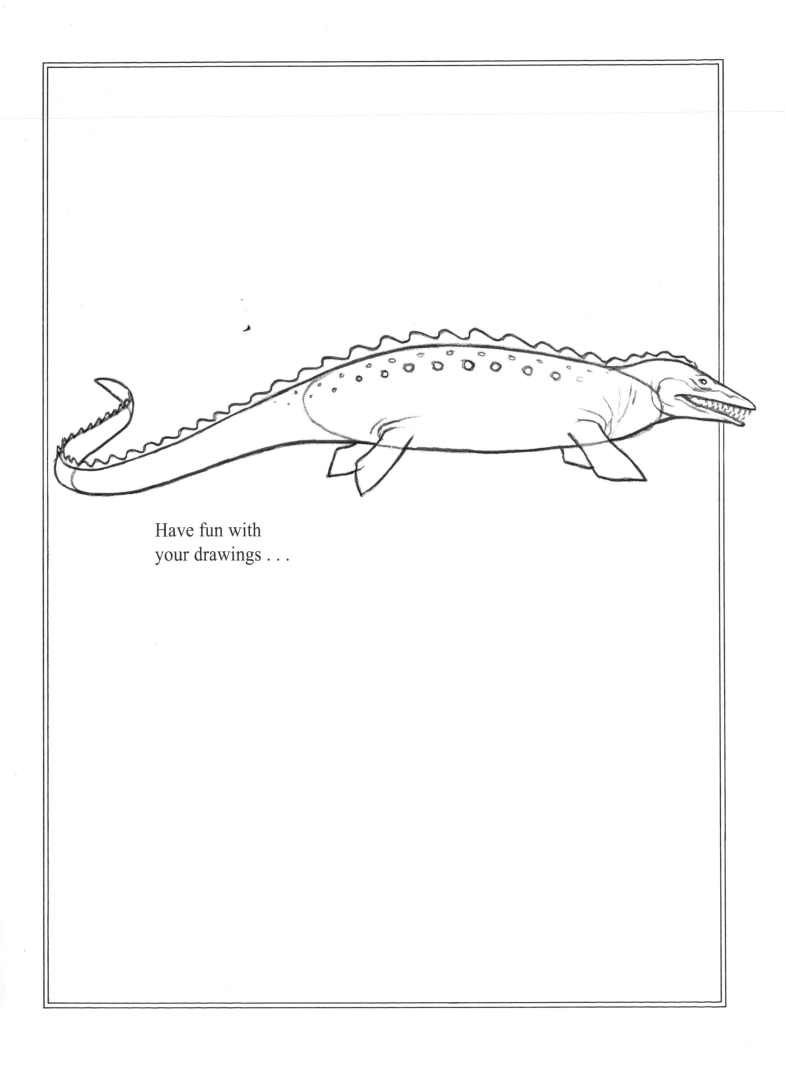

Have fun with
your drawings . . .

TYRANNOSAURUS 15 metres long
A giant meat-eating dinosaur

APATOSAURUS (formerly BRONTOSAURUS)   20 metres long
A plant-eating dinosaur

STEGOSAURUS 6 metres long
A plated dinosaur

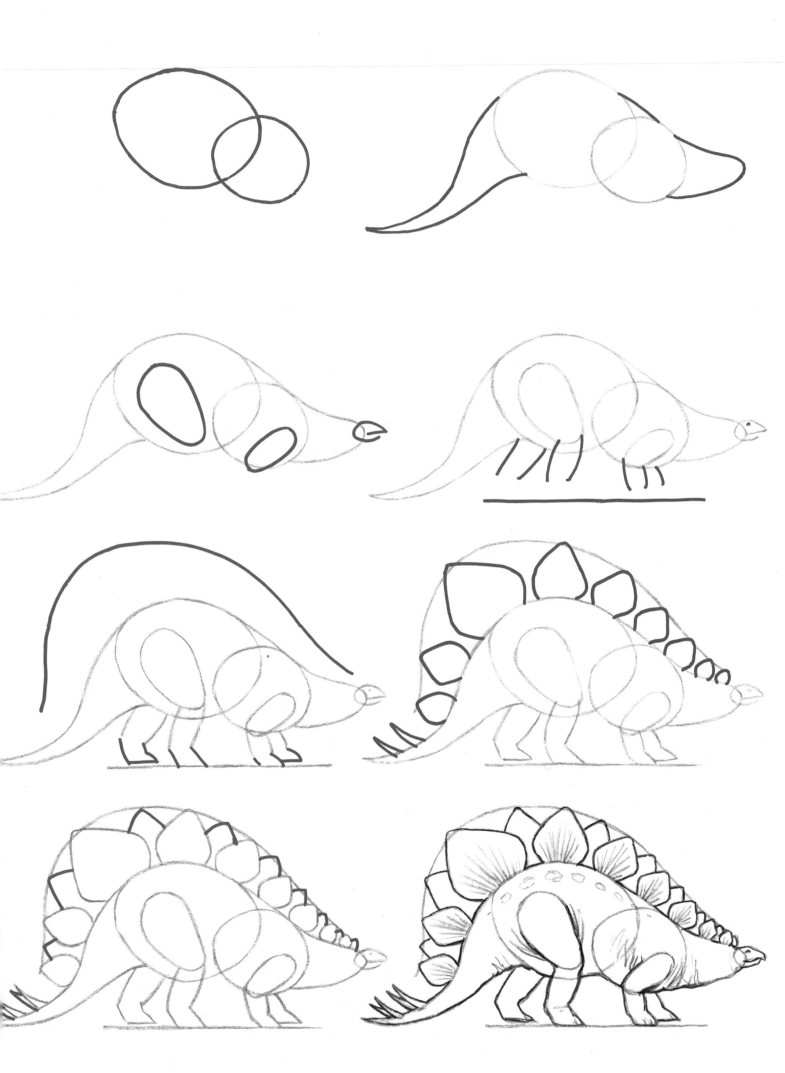

PROTOCERATOPS 2 metres long
An early horned dinosaur

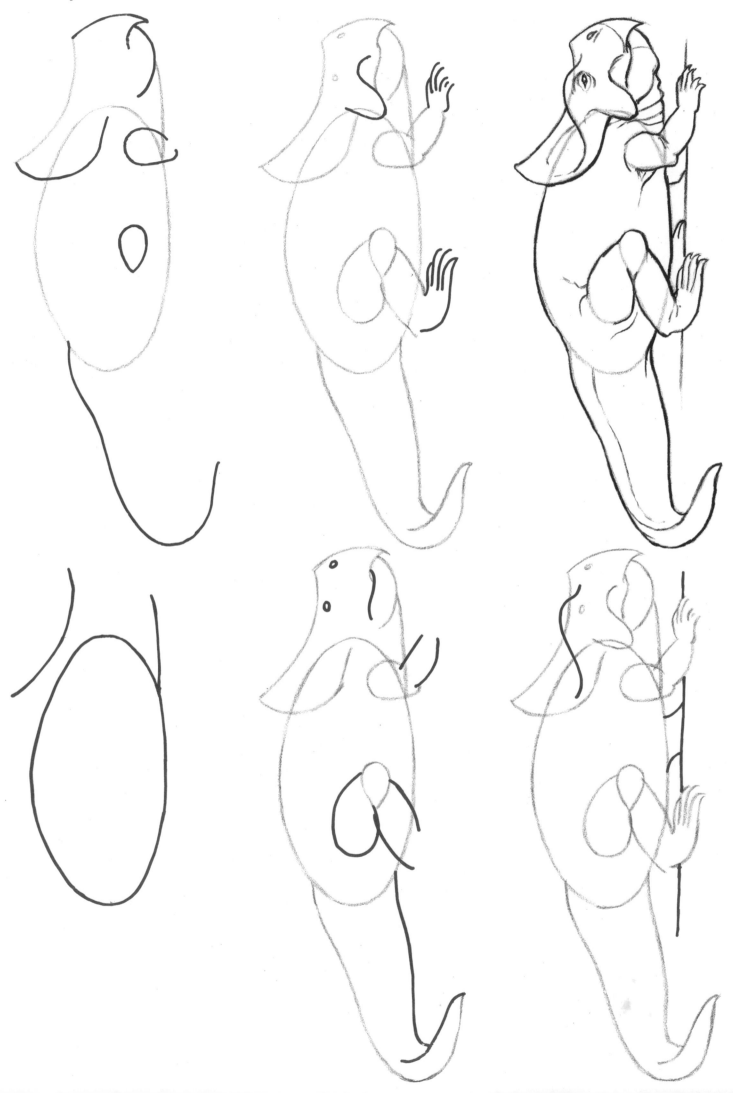

TRICERATOPS 9 metres long
A plant-eating horned dinosaur

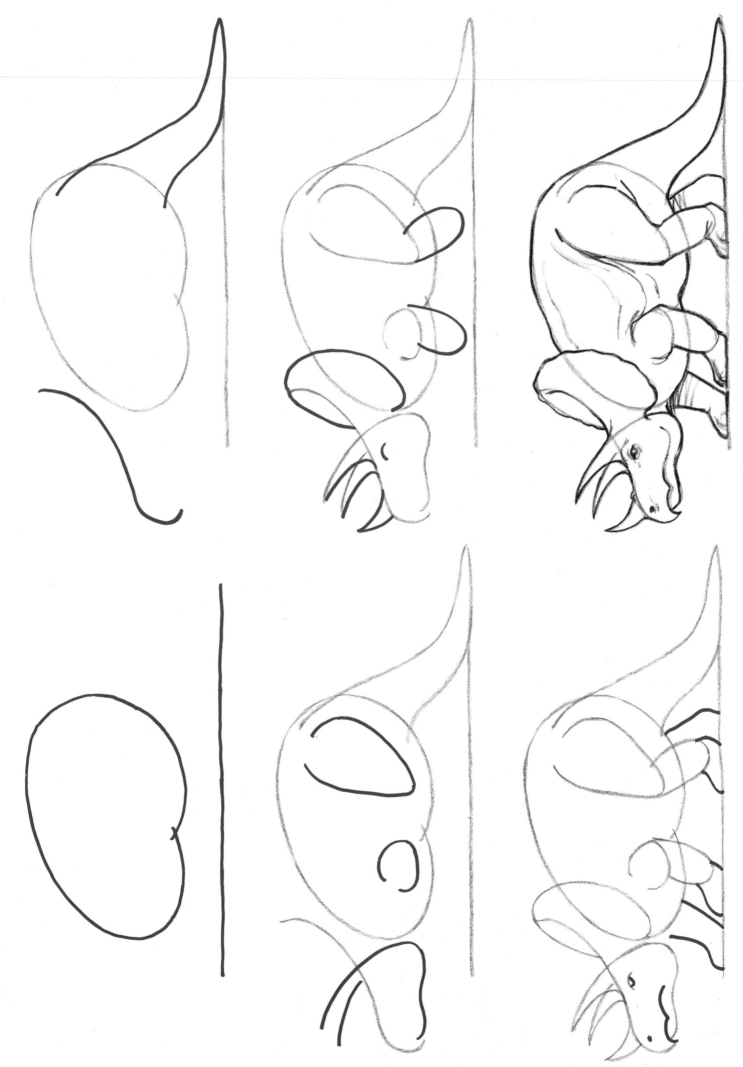

STYRACOSAURUS 5 metres long
A plant-eating horned dinosaur

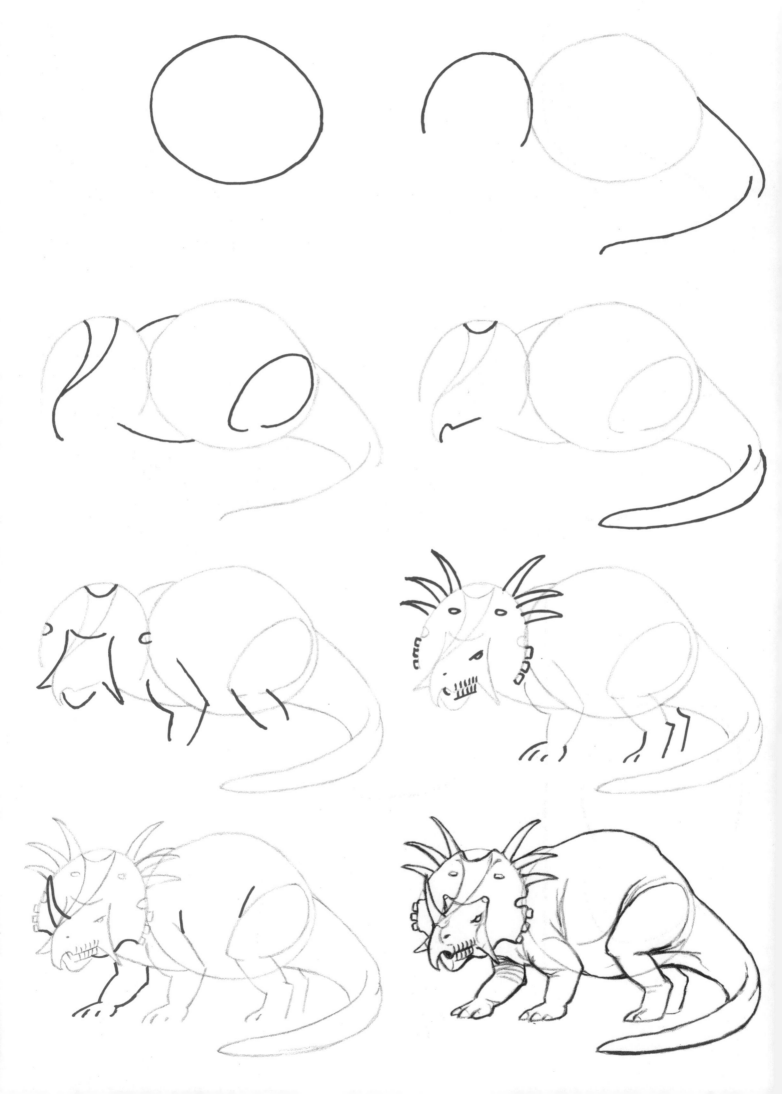

IGUANODON 9 metres long
A plant-eating dinosaur

ANKYLOSAURUS 6 metres long
A plant-eating armoured dinosaur

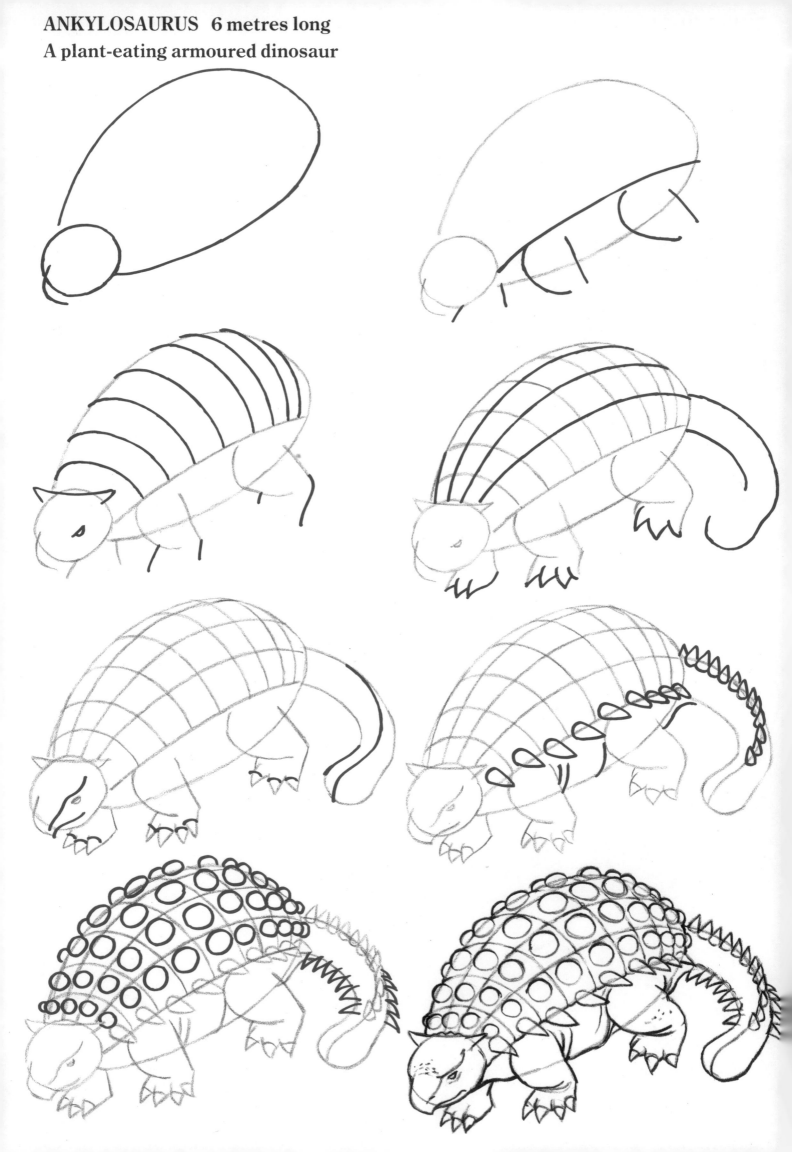

DIPLODOCUS 27 metres long
A giant plant-eating dinosaur

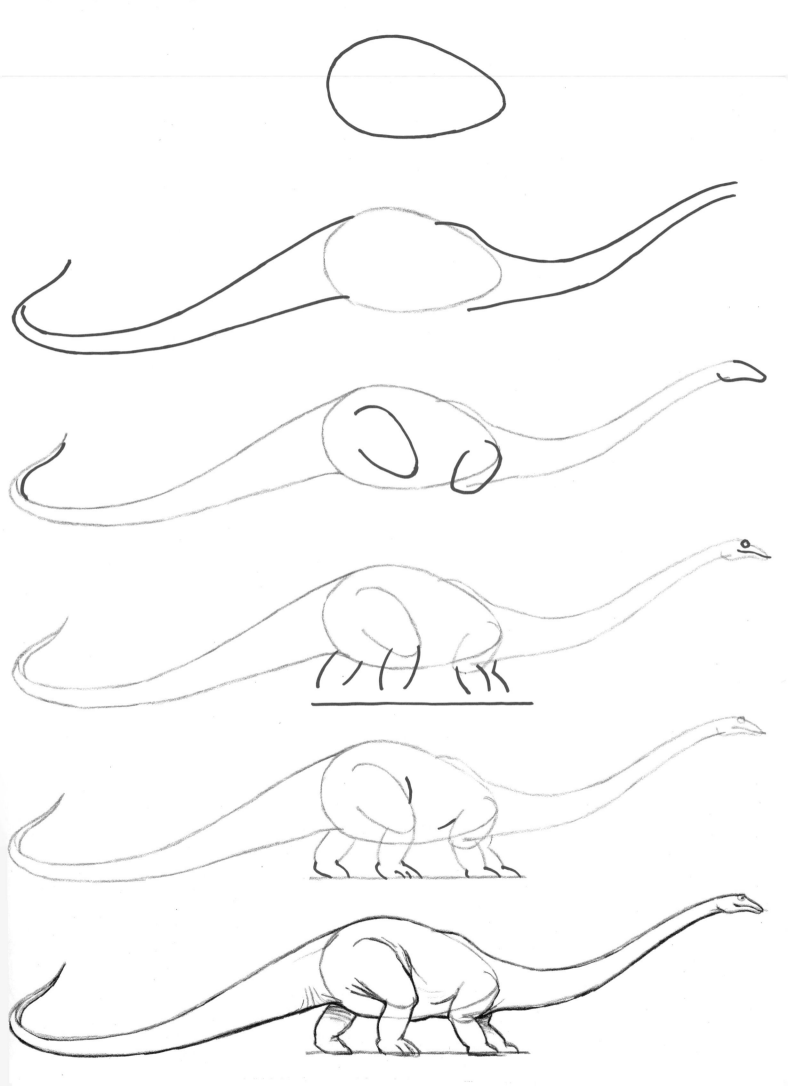

STRUTHIOMIMUS 2 metres tall
The 'Ostrich' dinosaur

BRACHIOSAURUS 12 metres tall
The bulkiest of the giant plant-eating dinosaurs

ANATOSAURUS 9 metres long
A duck-billed dinosaur

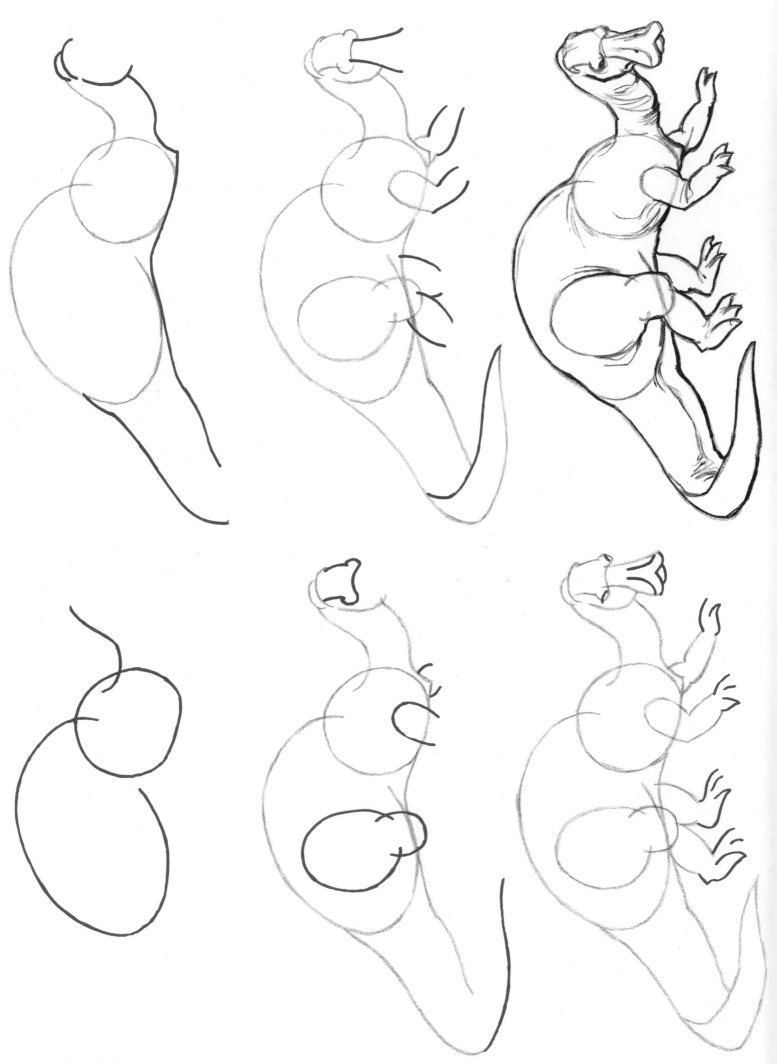

A NAUTILOID 3 metres long
An ancient relative of squids and octopuses

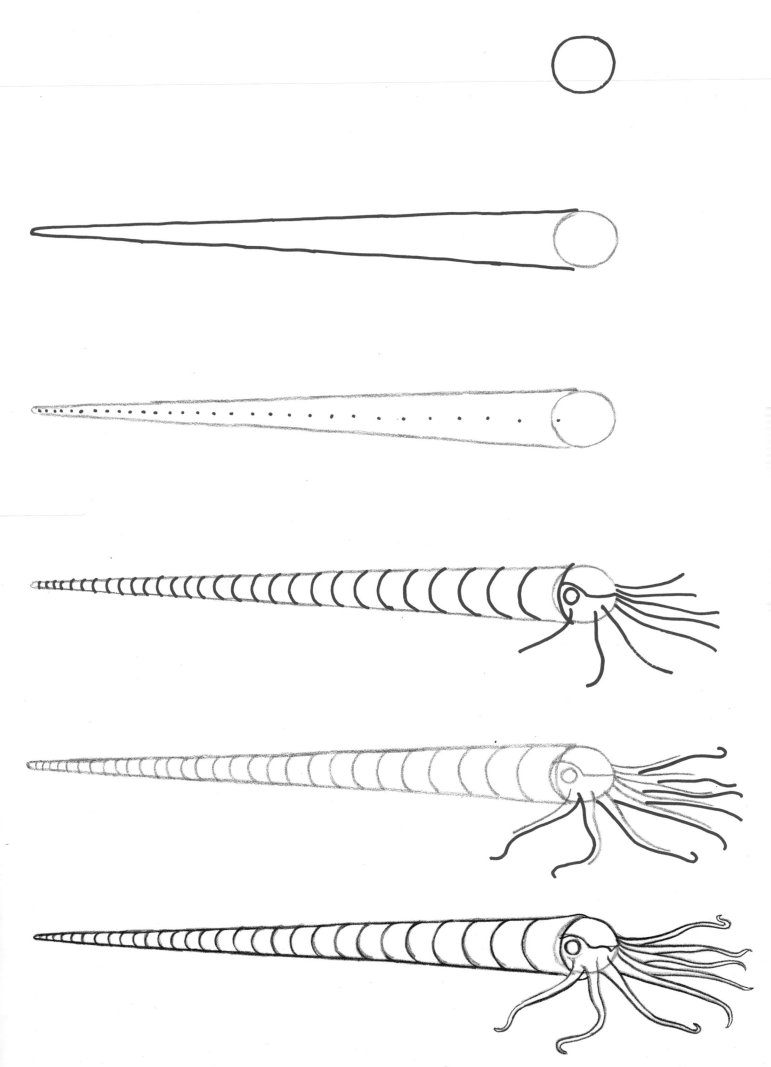

AN AMMONOID 13 centimetres long
An ancient mollusk

A TRILOBITE 10 centimetres long
An ancient relative of the crabs, spiders and insects

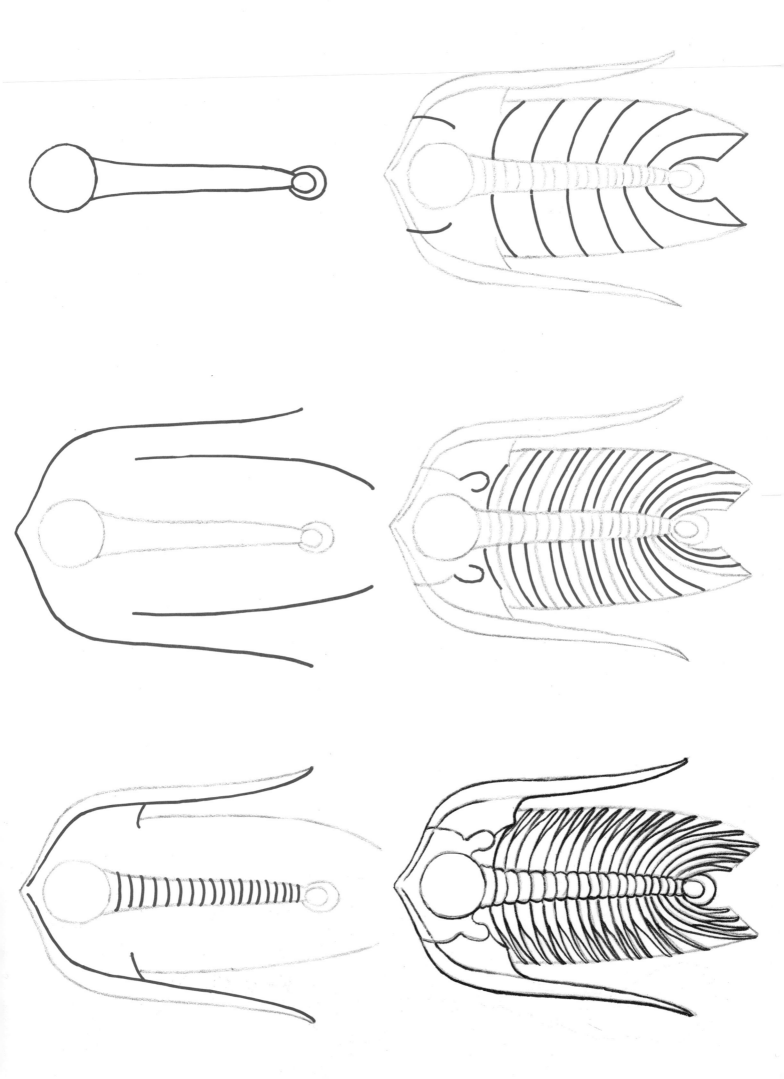

AN EURYPTERID 3 metres long
A seagoing relative of scorpions and spiders

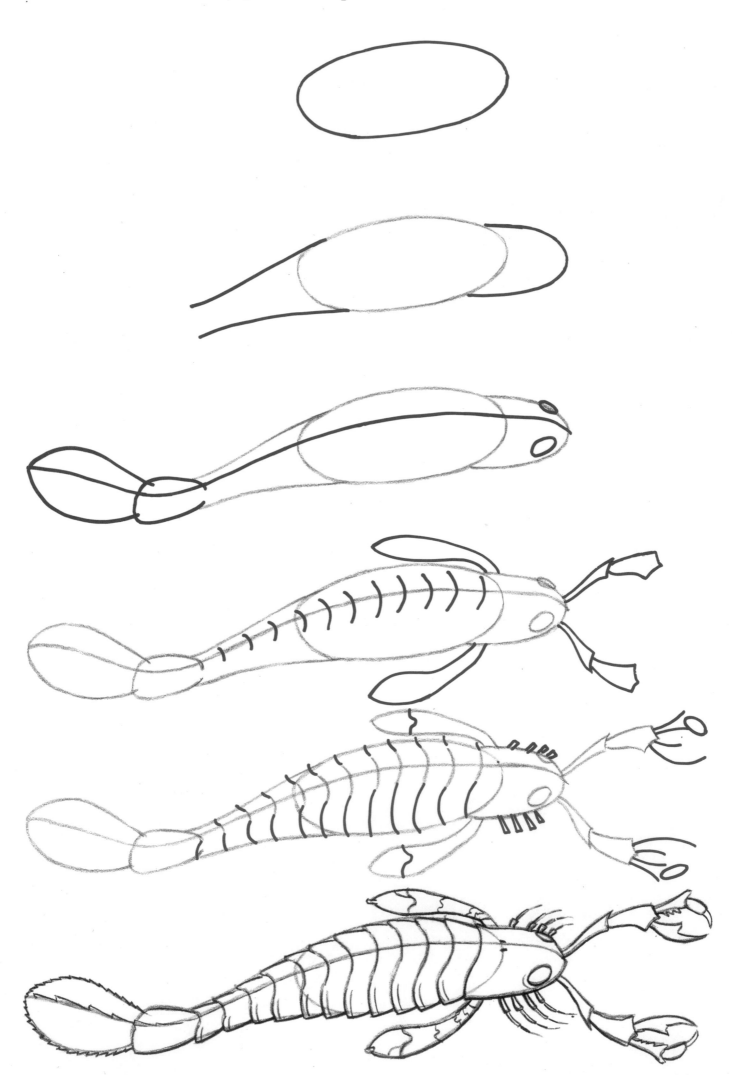

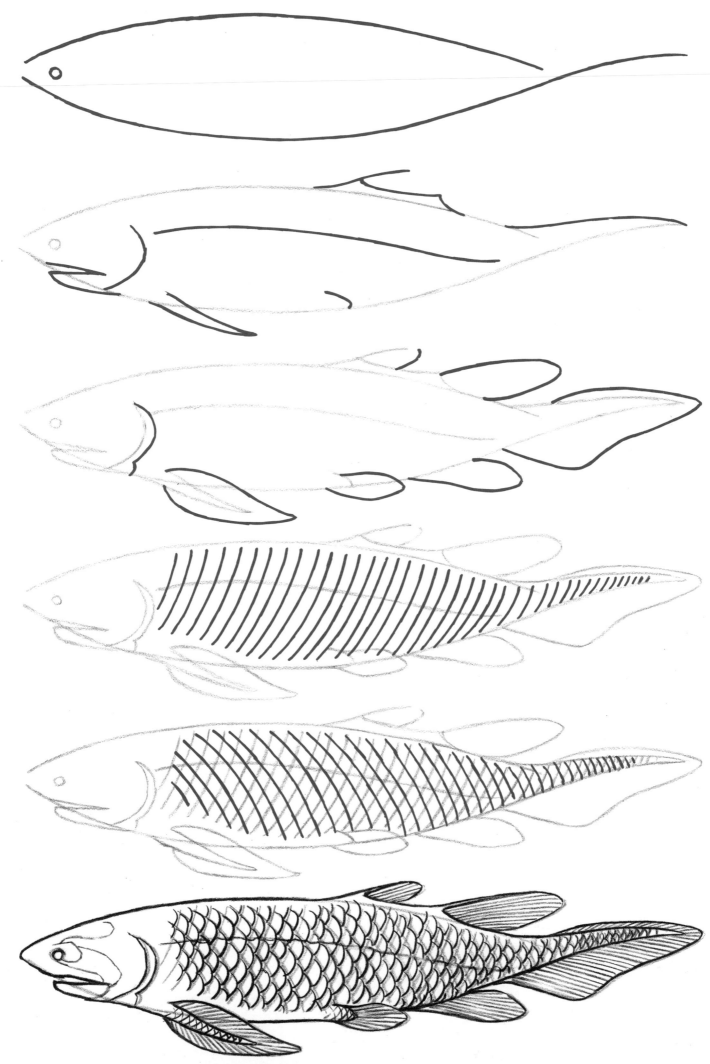

PLEURACANTHUS 2 metres long
A spiny fish – not related to the sharks

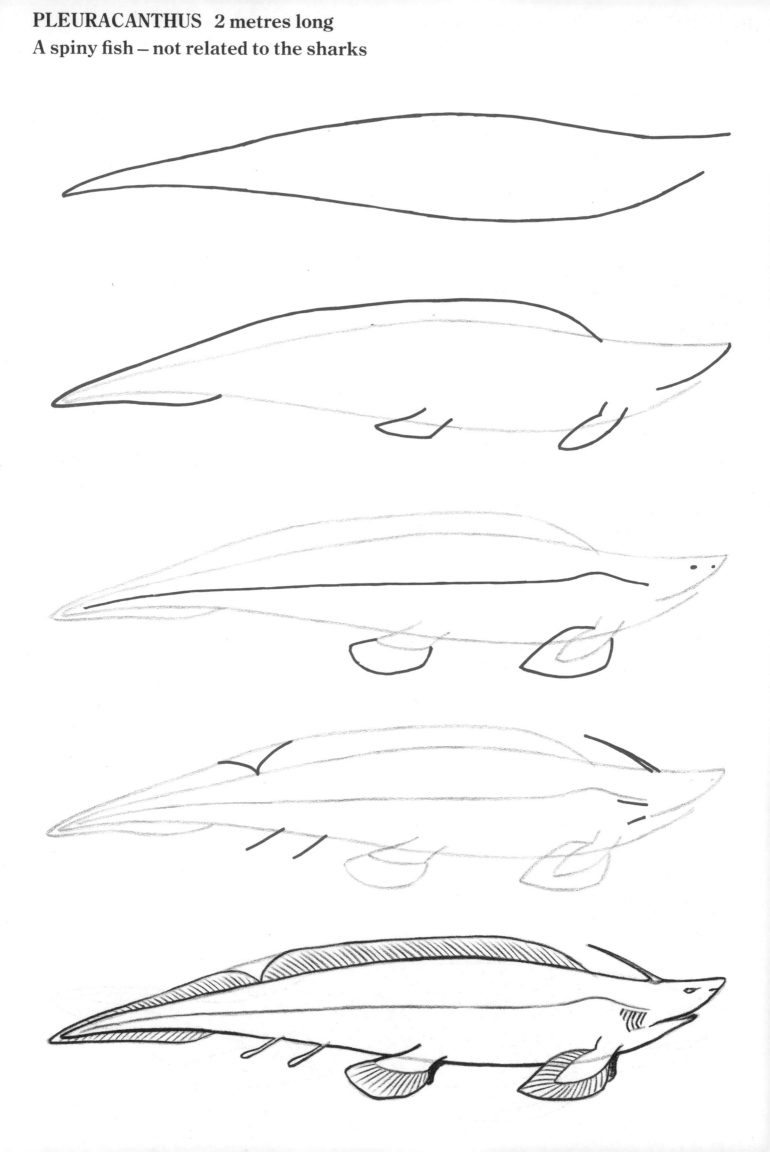

DINICHTHYS 9 metres long
An ancient giant fish

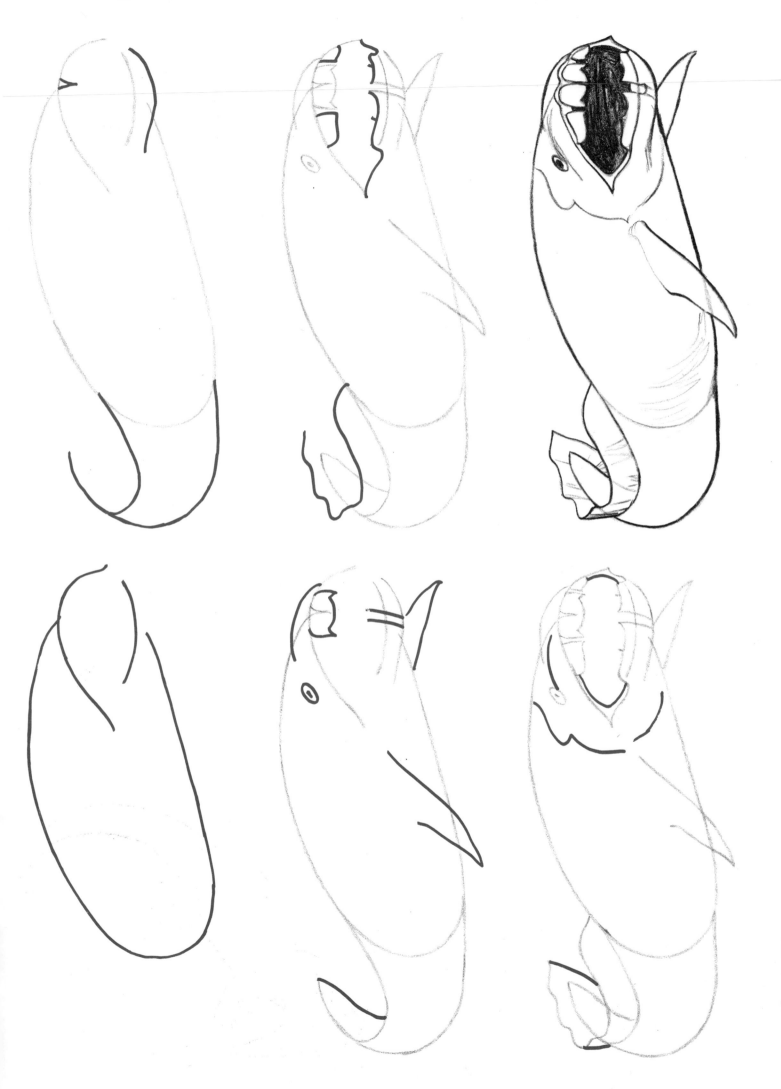

DIPLOCAULUS 60 centimetres long
An early water-living amphibian

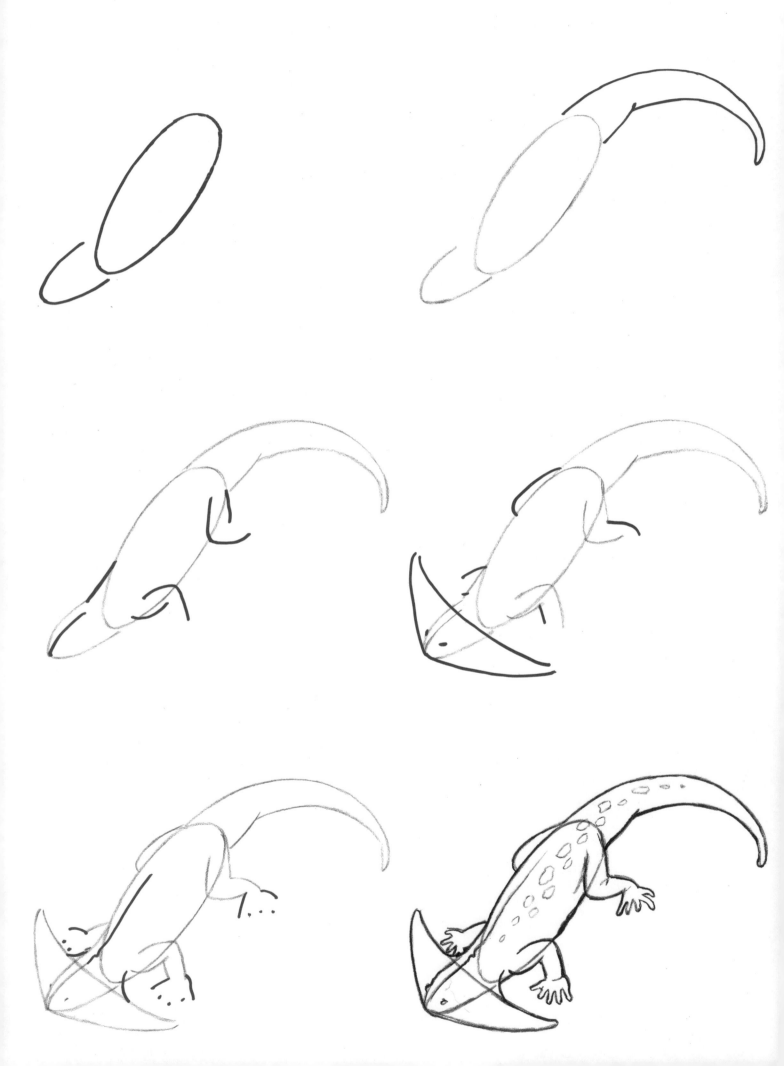

ERYOPS 1.5 metres long
An early land-going amphibian, distantly related to modern frogs

MESOSAURUS 40 centimetres long
Early fish-eating reptile

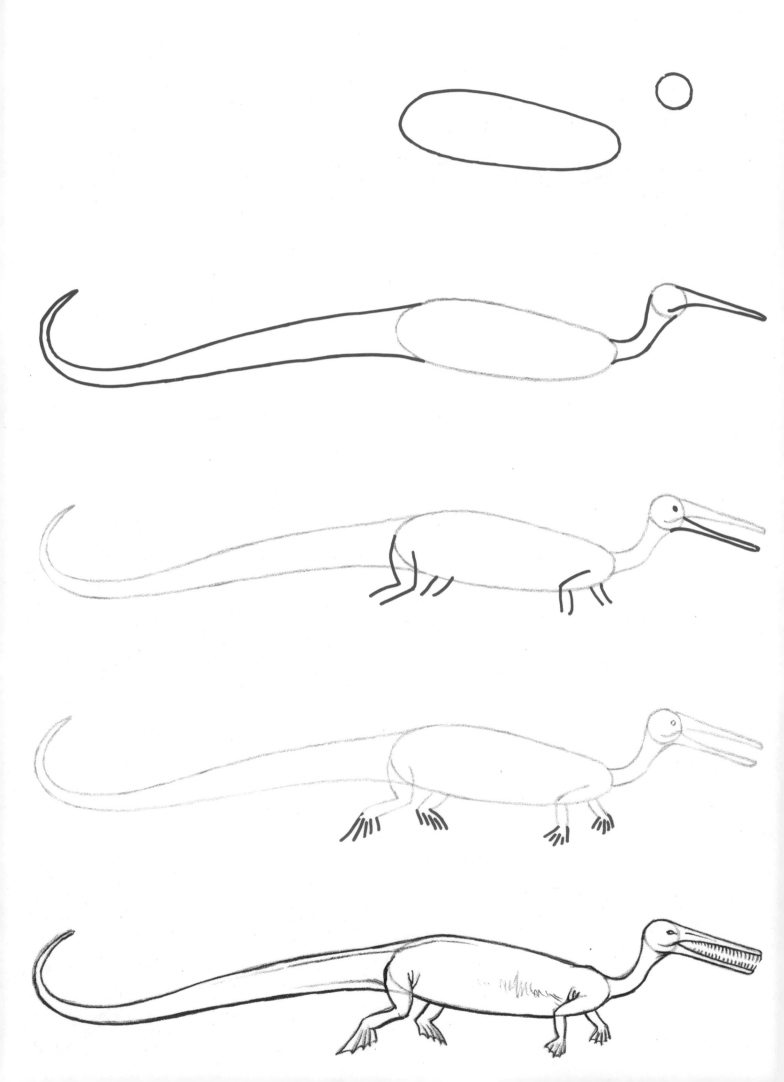

ICHTHYOSAUR 12 metres long
A seagoing reptile

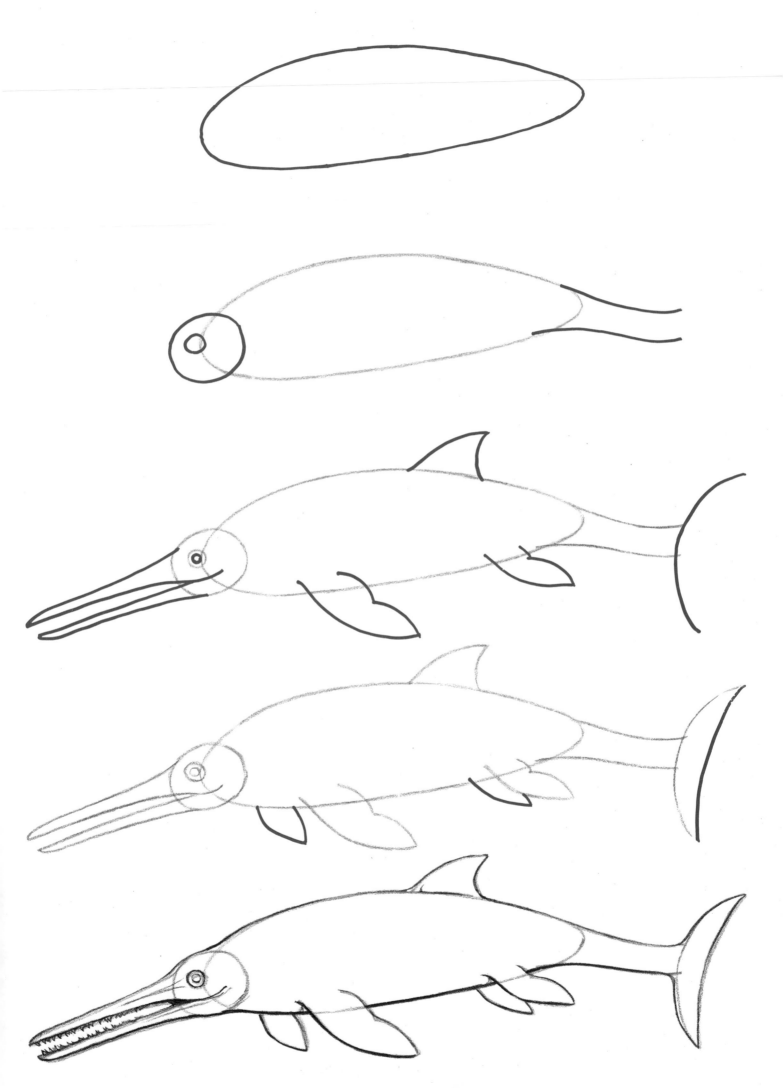

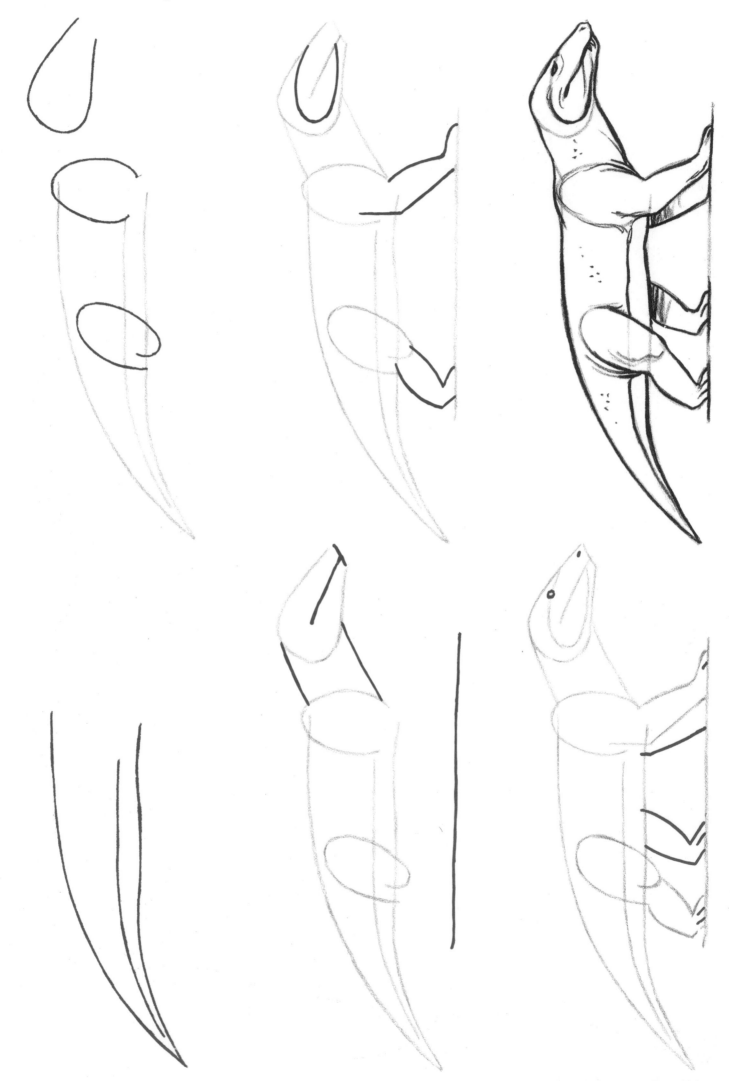

GEOSAURUS 5 metres long
A seagoing crocodilian

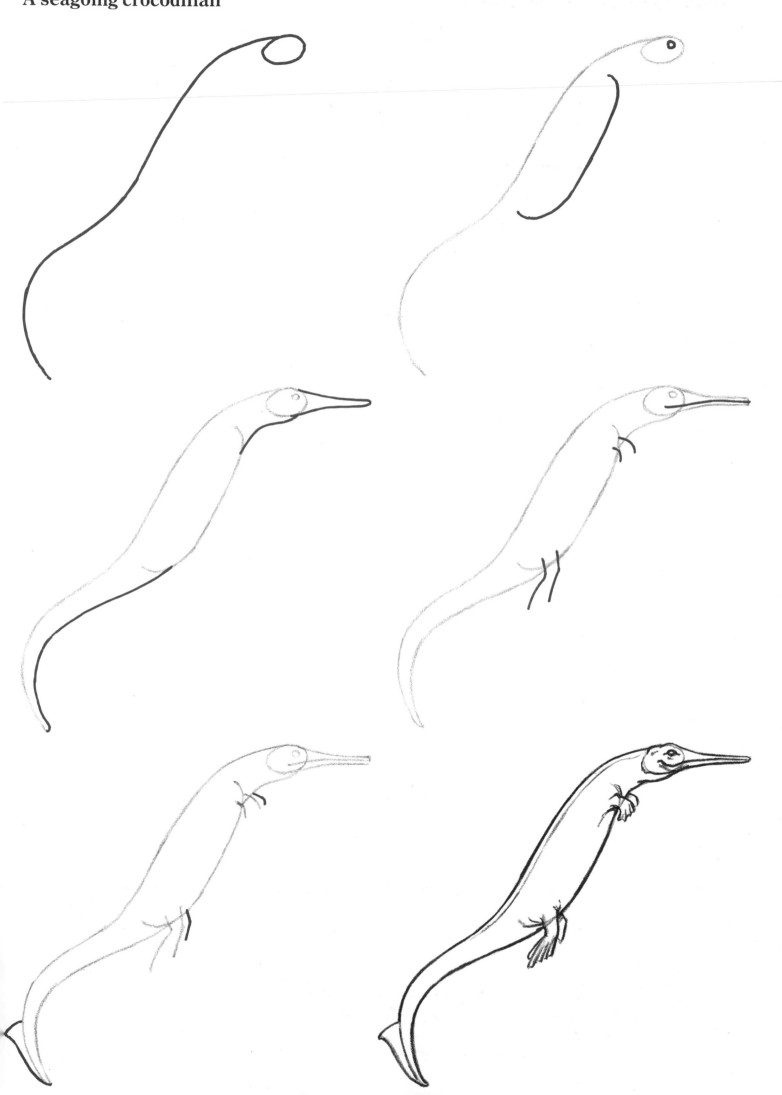

TRIMACROMERUM 3 metres long
A short-necked seagoing reptile

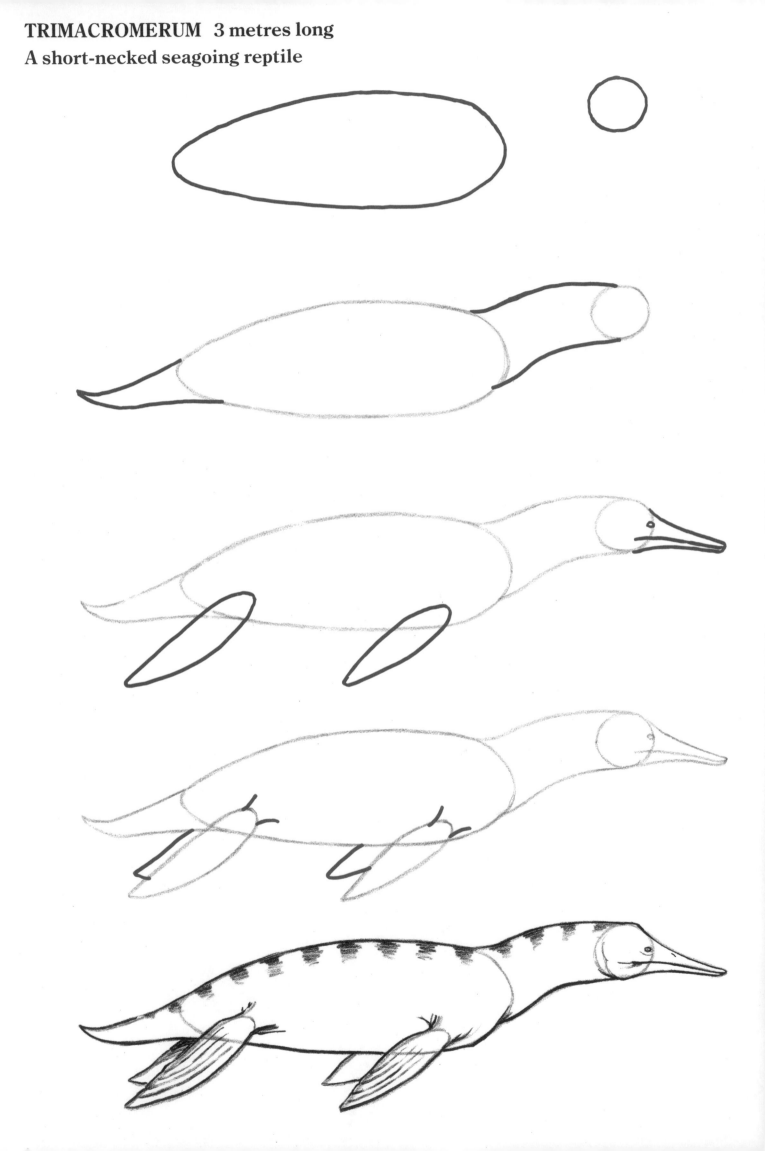

KANNEMEYERIA 2 metres long
A mammal-like reptile

ELASMOSAUR 15 metres long
A snake-necked sea reptile

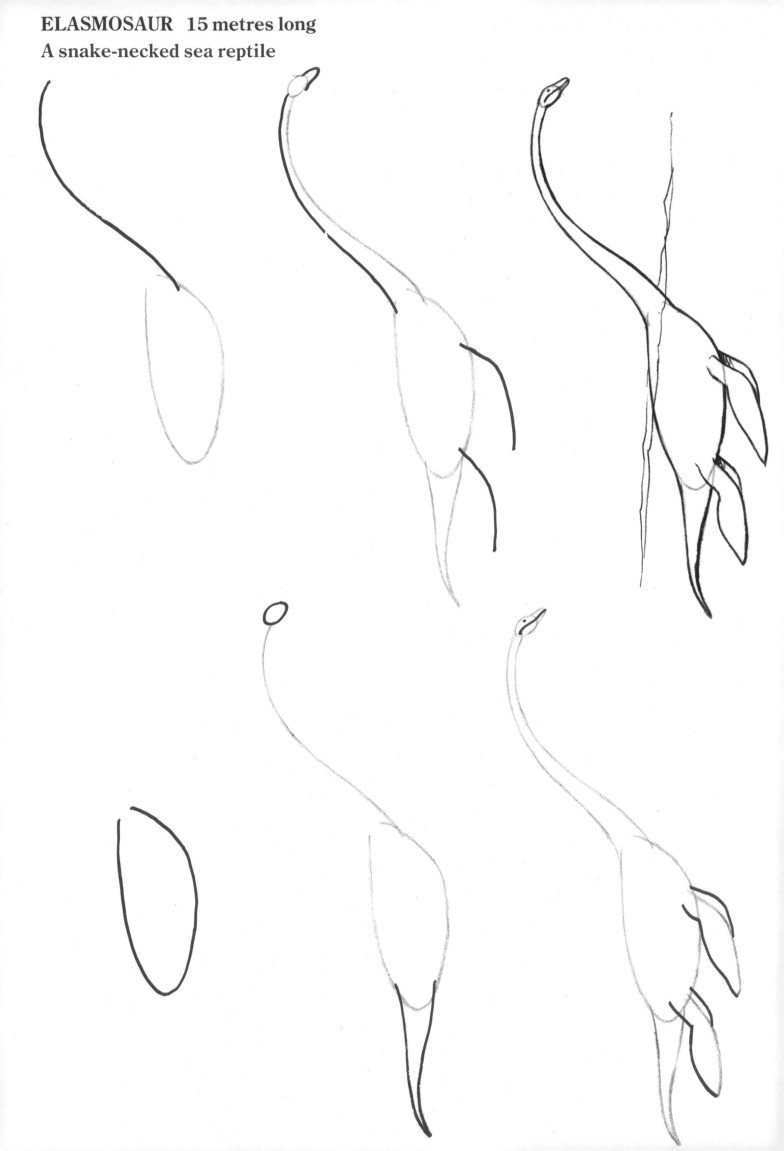

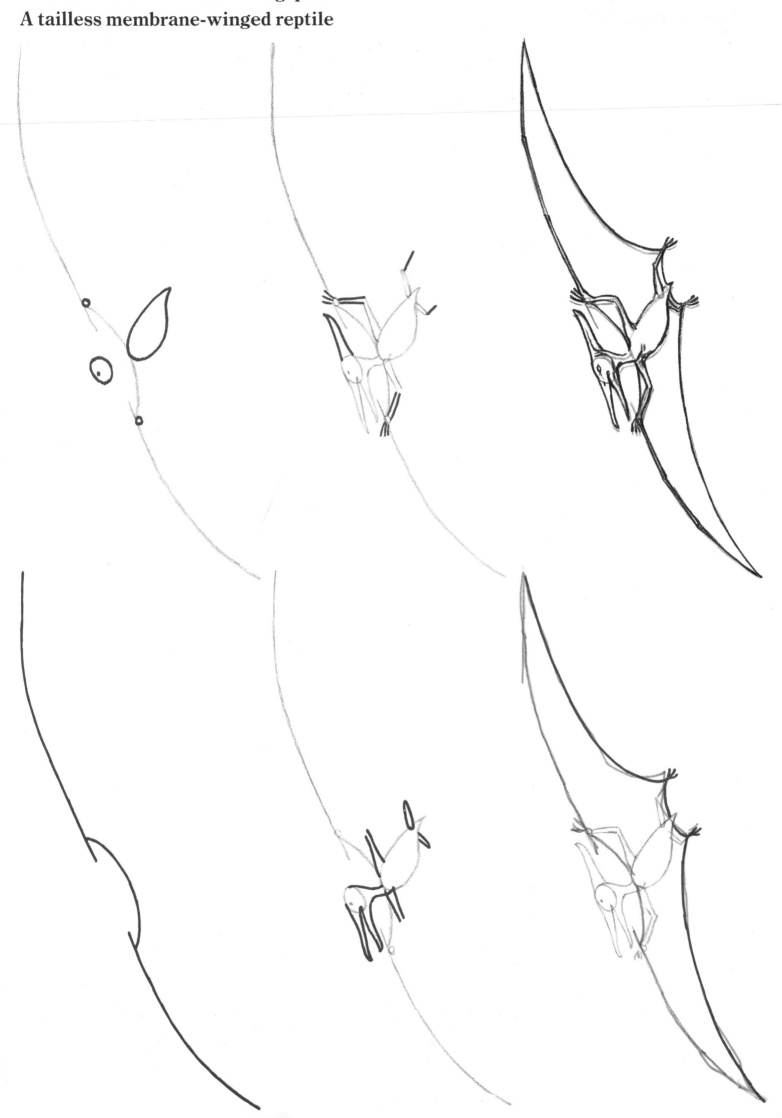

MOSASAUR 9 metres long
A seagoing lizard

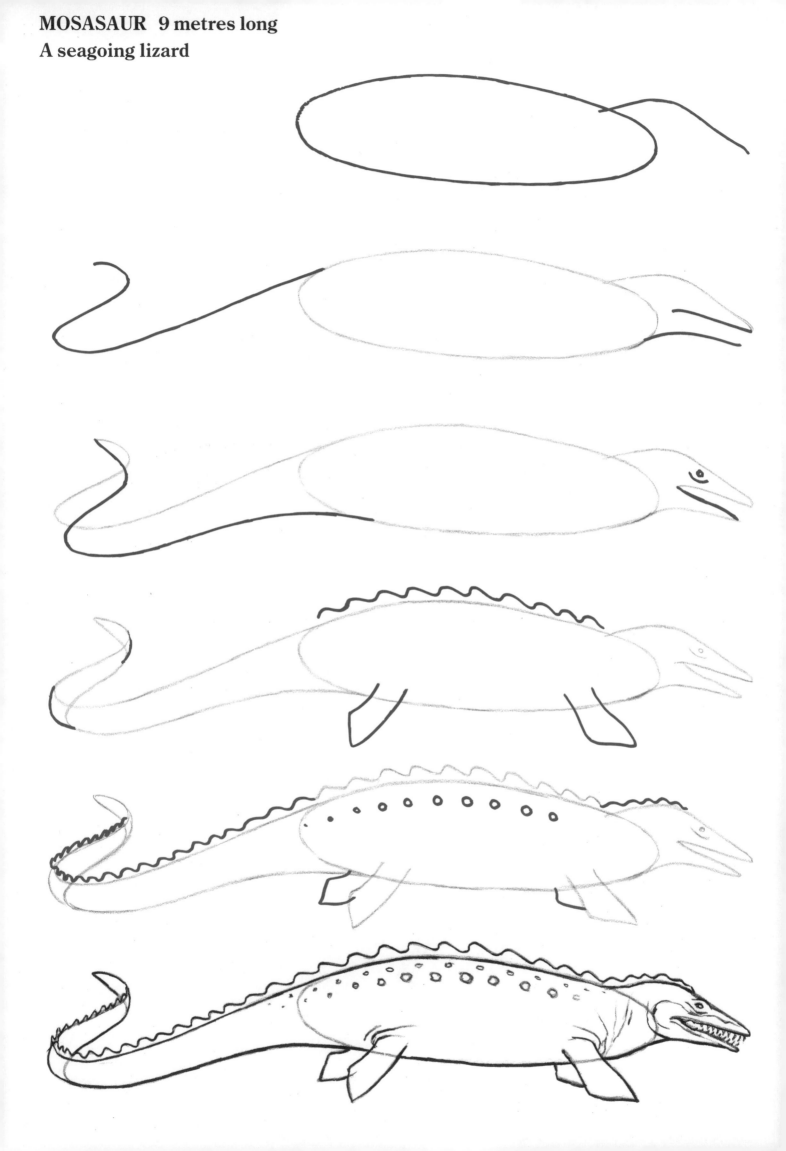

DIMETRODON 3 metres long
An early mammal-like reptile

ARCHELON 4 metres long
An ancient sea turtle

RHAMPHORHYNCHUS 1 metre long
A membrane-winged reptile

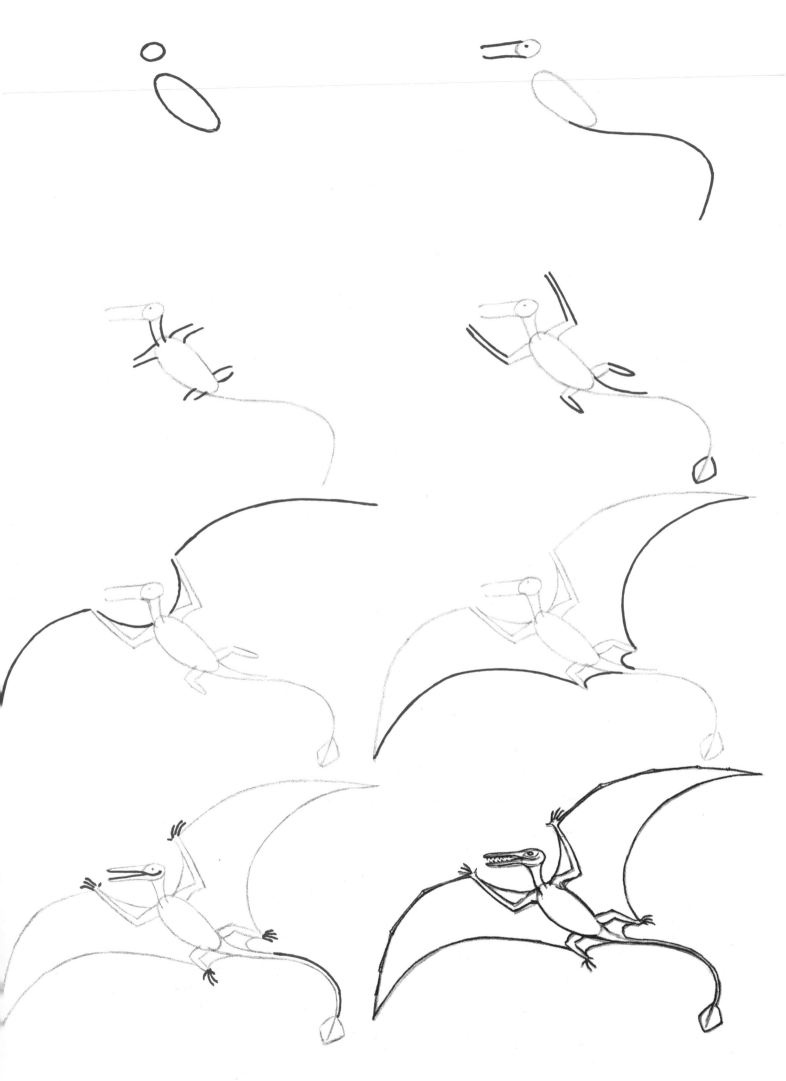

LONGISQUAMA 15 centimetres long
An early reptile

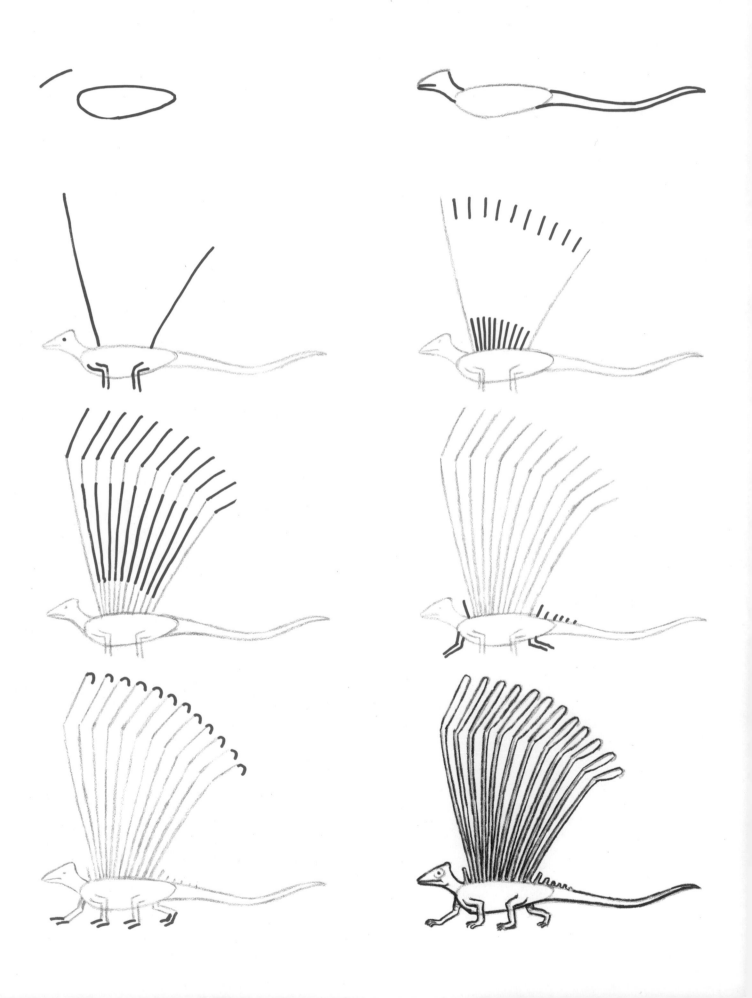

SALTOPOSUCHUS 1 metre long
A two-legged reptile, ancestor of dinosaurs and birds

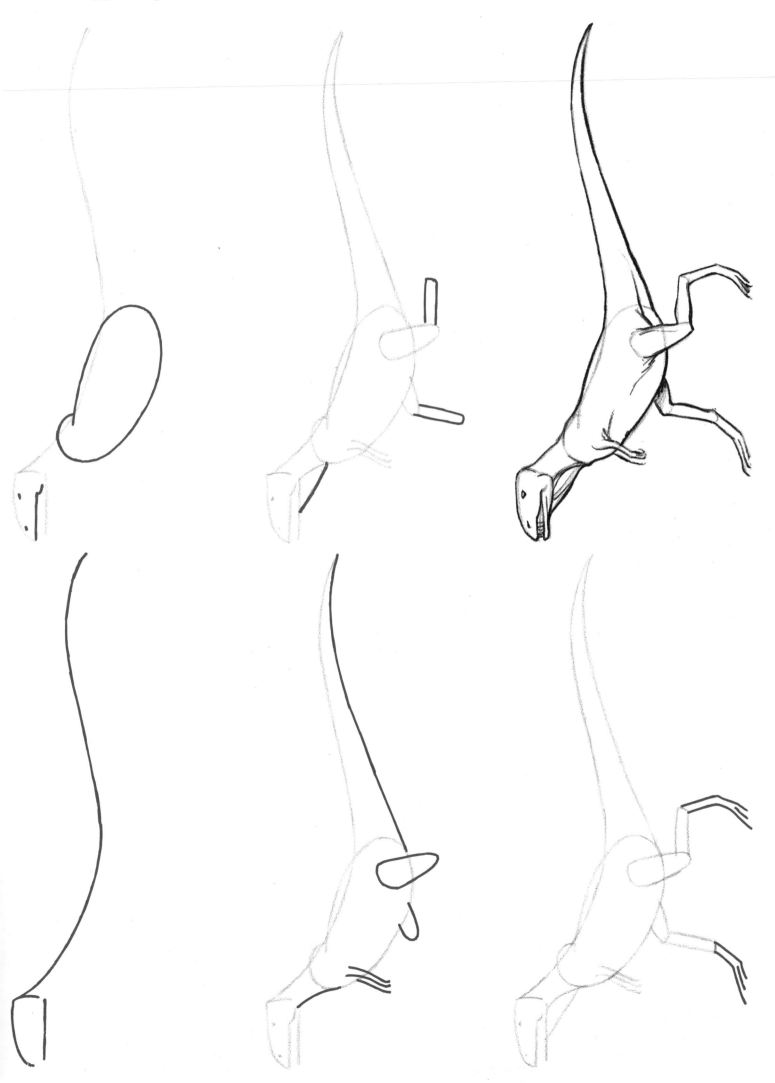

MOA 3 metres tall

A giant flightless bird of New Zealand

HESPERORNIS   1.5 metres tall
A primitive toothed diving bird

ARCHAEOPTERYX 38 centimetres long
The first bird

DIATRYMA   2 metres tall
A meat-eating giant flightless bird

SMILODON 2.5 metres long
A sabre-toothed cat

GLYPTODON 3 metres long
An ancient relative of the armadillo

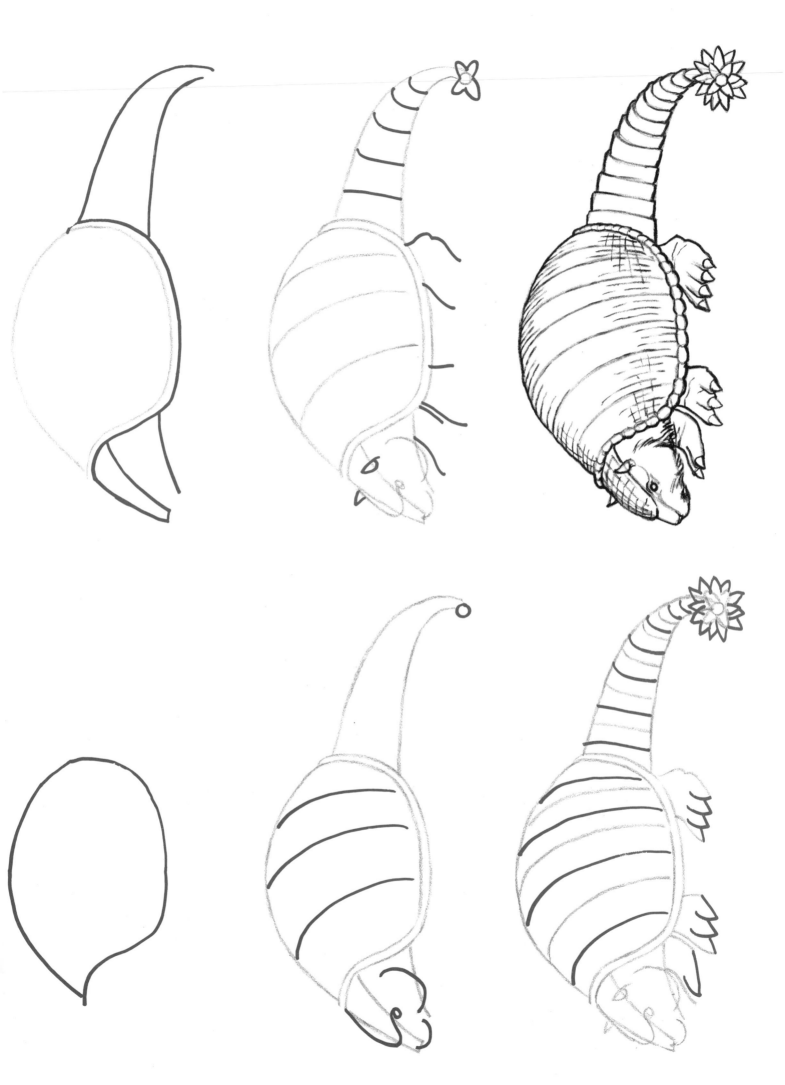

MEGALOCEROS 3 metres across the antlers
The giant elk of the Ice Age

ALTICAMELUS 5.5 metres tall
A giant camel

BALUCHITHERIUM 8 metres long
An ancient hornless rhinoceros

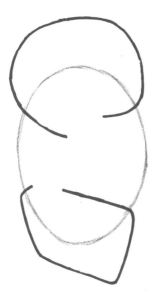

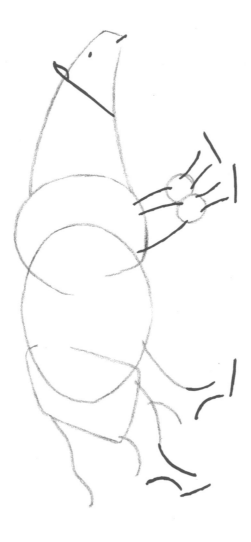

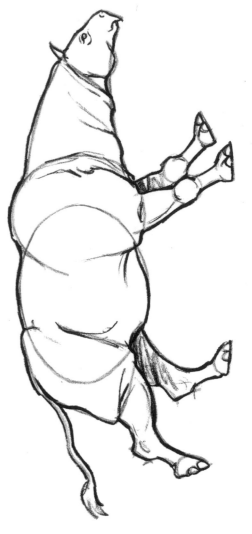

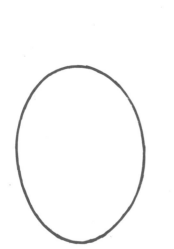

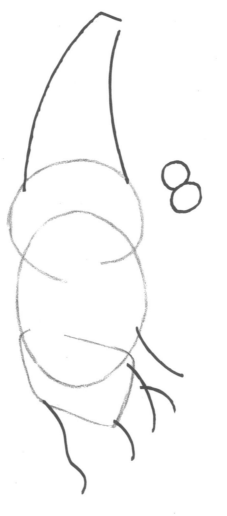

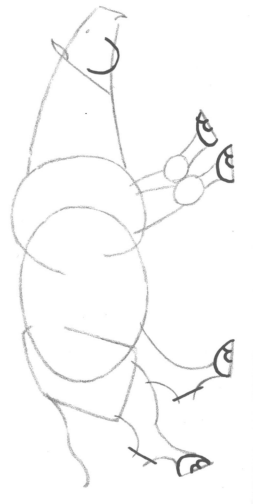

WOOLLY MAMMOTH   3 metres tall
An Ice Age elephant

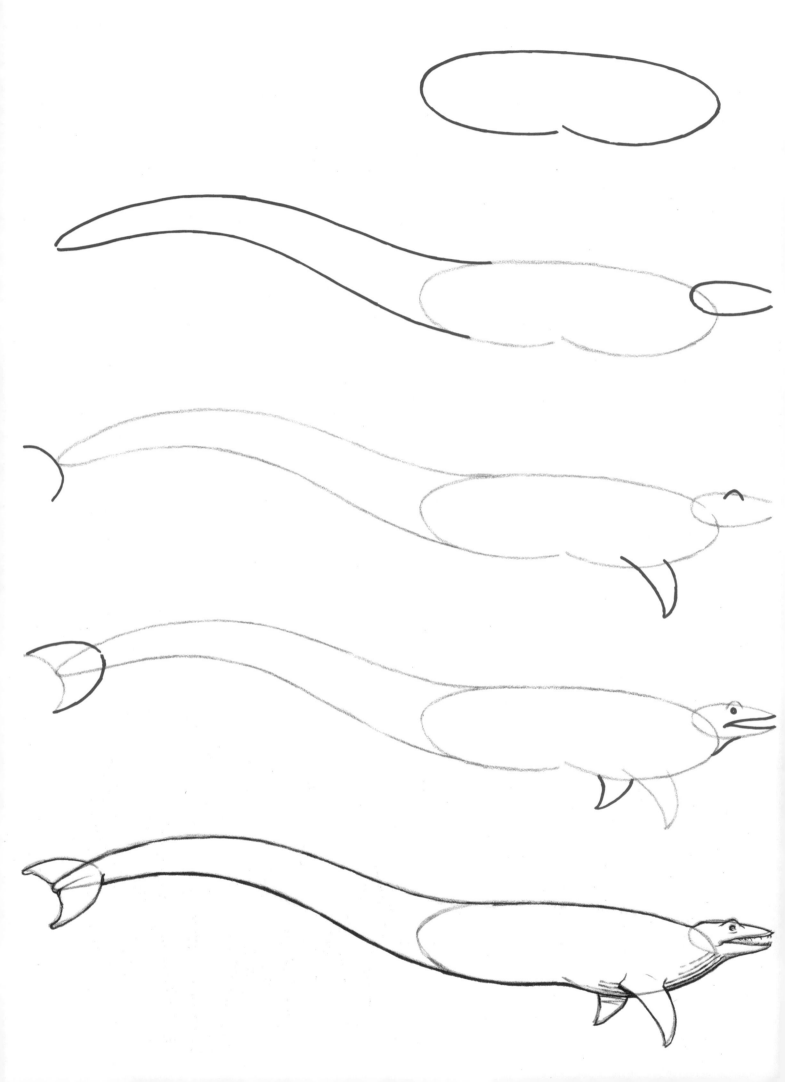

BRONTOTHERIUM 4.5 metres long
An early hoofed mammal, related to horses and rhinoceroses

MEGATHERIUM   7.5 metres long
A giant ground sloth

HYRACOTHERIUM (formerly EOHIPPUS)   45 centimetres long
The ancestor of the horse

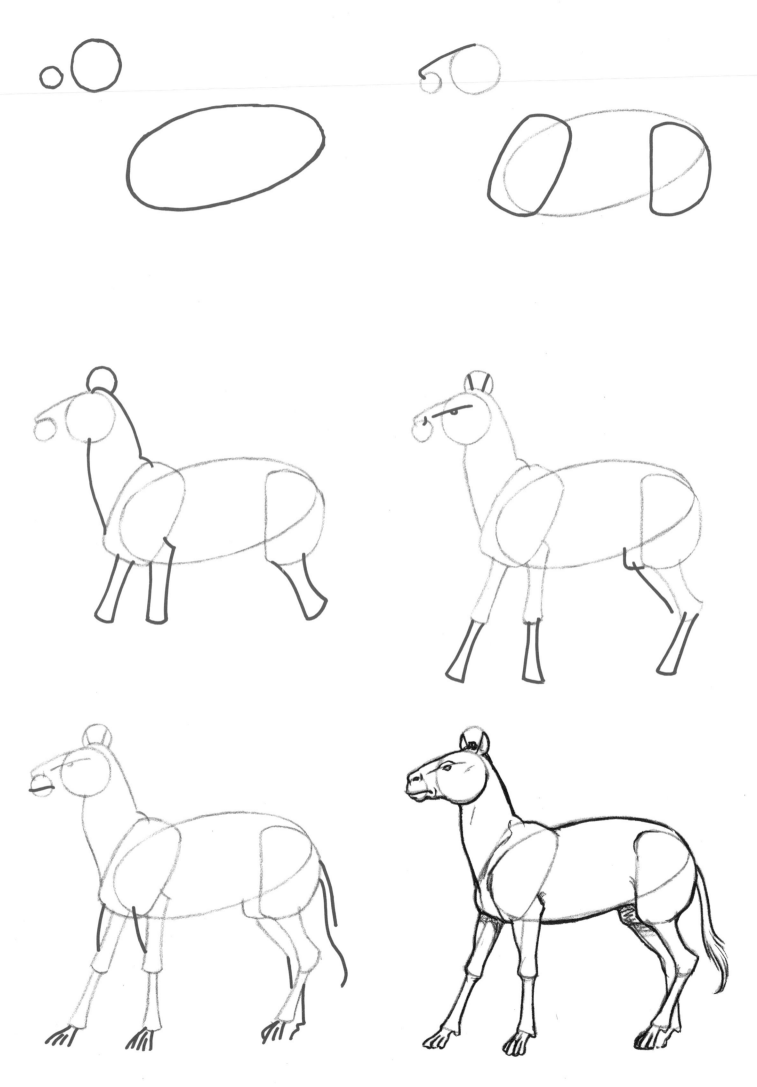

ABOUT THE AUTHOR

Lee J. Ames has been earning his living as an artist for almost forty years. He began his career working on Walt Disney's *Fantasia* and *Pinocchio*. He has taught at the School of Visual Arts in New York City and, more recently, at Dowling College on Long Island, New York State. He was, for a time, director of his own advertising agency and illustrator for several magazines. Mr Ames has illustrated over one hundred books, from preschool picture books to postgraduate texts. When not working, he battles on the tennis court. A native New Yorker, Lee J. Ames lives in Dix Hills, Long Island, with his wife, Jocelyn, their three dogs, and a calico cat.